Who Am I?

Mia A. Sims

DEDICATION

I dedicate this book to all of you who are fighting each day against forces you don't understand—against life's sometimes cruel circumstances. We lose ourselves in time, traveling through life's never-ending abyss. It's often hard to find yourself in the midst of so much chaos. I've been there, and I wanted to showcase that to the world... to you. You will overcome.

CONTENTS

ACKNOWLEDGMENTS

Acknowledgements are due to everyone who helped me through each troubling phase of my life. I am finally free and I owe it to my spiritual creator, all of you earthly angels that cared, and myself. A special thanks to J. Libertine for the book cover's illustration.

Thank you.

Chapter 1:
Darkness Falls

Sins of the Father Part 1

I think I was 12,
When I felt the first touch.
I was asleep, reclining deep,
On my best friend's sofa.
It startled me from my sleep.
Her father conveniently behind me,
Holding a drink.
As if he'd come to my rescue…
He'd heard me coughing like crazy,
And though my mind was so hazy.
The next day, I remembered it all.
Those nights I'd written off,
As terrible nightmares,
My thoughts were false.
I'd been assaulted repeatedly—
Over and over in my sleep.
I was sick. Why him?
And God, why me?
I maybe told a few souls.
I mean, I was only 12-years-old…
And my friend told me
It happened to her, too.
It hurt, but you see,
It wasn't just me.
I wasn't alone.

One moment...
Just a few seconds…
Ruining me within forever,
I'll never be the same.

Alone

Sailing without direction,
Yearning for affection,
She wanders with no fear,
Diving through life,
Not shedding a tear.
Until she's alone,
Alone in the dark,
No one near to hear.
But her heart,
That's when it happens,
The realization of winning,
of losing,
Of failing,
always trying,
She's crying.
He's lying,
But so is she.
To herself, to the world,
Alone in the dark...

It was at the age of 12,
That I made the first incision.
I contemplated for awhile
Before I made my final decision.
It would only get worse…
As the pain grew deeper.
14-years-old,
knives, scissors, blades,
Slowly digging deeper.
It felt much bearable this time…
A pain that I enjoyed.
I questioned my sanity…
But I didn't feel I had a choice.
And maybe it was in my mind,
But I could've sworn I heard a voice say,
"Better luck next time."
As if it was wishing me away.
A darkness was reigning deep…
And each day it spoke.
Whispers of worthlessness,
Suicide… I didn't see hope.
I cut through high school,
On into college.
It was the act of a known stranger,
Who would eventually
make me stop it.

Deliver me

How many cuts
Does it take to feel?
How many days
Would it take to heal?
Why do I feel
That I'm in this alone?
Screaming for help,
No place to call home.
I asked for advice,
I was told to pray.
I then asked why—
"Don't question your faith."
So here I am again,
Cutting … on the verge of sin.
I need deliverance.
Just let me in.

Mary

It was a Wednesday
In September,
A day I'll always remember.
She was celebrating her birthday.
I almost forgot to call.
But in the midst of my high,
I began to fall.
For an hour we talked and laughed.
But it was late…I had class…
"Well I have to go grandma,
I'll see you next—
She didn't want to leave
Should've known it was strange.
A coma by Friday…
I felt somewhat deranged.
Her voice still so clear.
If I strain enough…
I can hear.
I wanted you to wake up.

I think I want an escape,
A way to end it all.
I don't want to hear a voice.
Not a single call.
Take away my indiscretions,
Take away the crippling pain.
Take away my livelihood…
Take away my name.

She has no fear of the future
That energy is for the past.
Hates herself for the mistakes.
The pain will always last.
She looks at herself in the mirror.
To herself pleading her case.
Just to be reminded of the pain,
The stranger staring back at her face.
Life isn't worth living.
But she lives anyway.
Constantly cutting her wrist,
Wishing life away.

Depression

Tell me where do you go—
When hell is all you know?
Walking completely blind
Trying to erase the thoughts
But they won't clear your mind.
Soft whispers encouraging to kill,
This evil state of mind.
Just doesn't seem real.
Who understands—
What is diagnosed as insanity?
Fighting to be common
Just as the rest of humanity.
Make it stop.
Slowly rip it from my head.
So that once it's gone,
It will surely remain dead.

I'm praying.
Please save me.
I'm on my last
Inch of grace.
I am screaming—
Bleeding inside.
I want away
From this place.

They called me everything,
But a saint or child of God.
I remember my own friends,
Turning their noses,
Refusing a nod.
I had family spread lies.
There was never any truth.
I lost myself in their words.
I was slowly losing my youth.
If only they knew,
The trials that I endured.
I never spoke a word.
My humbleness reassured.
In a place of darkness,
It's hard to pay attention.
Their words cut deep, though.
They forced these afflictions.

Love, hope
Hell, despair.
Searching for redemption
But no redeemer is near.
Calling to the dark,
Encouraging demons to enact.
Preparing to battle,
Only to never react.
Promises, care,
Why were you never there?
Desolation, the cold…
Why do you remain in my soul?

Cry child cry…
For only you
Can hear yourself weep.
Child child cry…
I know the mountains
Have gotten so steep.
Cry child cry,
Tell the story of a lost soul.
Tell of the sight of horror
That made you so cold.
Cry child cry…
If no one hears you, I can.
Only because those tears,
Are right in the palms of my hands

They say time brings about a change.
So please tell me where is mine.
I keep doing the same things,
Each time with a colder set mind.
I grow more hollow each time.
If only I could go back,
Yeah I'd change a few things…
I'm not happy with what happened…

I was blind,
The sublime,
Was my hand of defense.
I danced in the rain.
Slowly losing the sense.
To feel, to touch,
We all want to belong.
I danced in the rain,
Wishing to return home.

1-5-12
I live in a box.
I peep to discover a girl—
Rotting in misery.
She knows nothing that life has in store.
Tears swell each day
And no one knows.
Who would care?
She holds what
Could change her life forever.
Crying hysterically,
She throws it down.
I am moved—
To a place where there is joy.
I see the same girl,
Yet much older
She no longer cries.
She writes, then sings.
Life is finally worth living.
One knock at the door,
One shot.
It ends.

1-6-12
From the depths of an unknown world,
It slowly rises, searching for its prey.
From tunnels below streets,
To alleys kept hushed
From the children of priests.
Creeps slowly from the closet
Watches them sleep.
Dares them to open their eyes.
Maneuvers its wrath,
Into the mind of the innocent.
Rips them of purity—
Forcing a soul of sin
Desperate for the kill.

The door is closed
But the curiosity within me
Begged to creep.
A cloud of fog welcomes me.
I slam it shut, yet still curious…
Slowly reopening, I see a light.
But not just any kind…
It held joy.
As I approached the warmness
It gave me hope.
For what exactly I don't know…
Closing my eyes,
I stretch my hand forward.
Something grabs me and lures me in.
I no longer feel the warmth.
As I open my eyes to face the coldness
That now conceals my hand,
I see the collage of everything
I've tried to forget.
There's no running away.
It's there forever.

1-5-12
I live in a box,
Though I frequently fly for amusement.
From the world of giants,
I enter a small structured place…
Where there lies a frightened giant…
Unlike any I've ever seen…
It releases water from small, rounded eyes...
It speaks, to itself, though I don't understand the
words.

The Running Man

Once there was a scared little boy
Who didn't like the Running Man.
He liked sports and food,
And girls and shoes…
And life and school…
But he didn't like the Running Man.
He pretended that his world was perfect.
When he hurt someone "they deserved it"
Yet not seeing the hold of the Running Man.
He played around in school.
Though following all the rules.
"laugh to keep from crying," he said.
Not escaping the Running Man.
His fear he couldn't admit,
So he lost all of it.
The one it took forever to get…
Problems caused by the Running Man.
The resentment won't go away,
Until forgiveness in your heart takes place.
Everything that makes you happy will go to waste—
All because of the Running Man.
Just keep in mind how he's made you feel,
In time your heart will heal…
Never let yourself become like him
Do all that you can…
Just please never become the Running Man.

Brown Eyes

His brown eyes sang a song,
That wouldn't cease.
They were flowing and rolling,
Fooling me.
I heard a whisper from his lips,
But I couldn't decipher.
I took hits for the trips,
All taking me higher.
I know I'm gullible,
But would you know
That I could sustain?
Lost in his brown eyes,
I remembered my name.
The Pied Piper told me yes,
All I wanted was no.
Lost in his eyes now,
I know trouble will follow,

Who Am I?

The more there's hate,
The more there's love.
I pull harder,
You continue to shove.
I cry, you don't.
I try, you won't.
The moment I smile,
You turn it around.
Are you doing it on purpose?
Guess I'll see in a while.
So much convincing,
From me to myself.
But my hope is sinking.
I just need your help.
Wish I would open
My eyes to see,
The only person
Who really cares,
Is me.

Let me breathe,
Let me live,
Let me give,
Everything…
To someone who means nothing
To someone who doesn't know me.

Just want to move away.
So far I'm forgotten.
So far not a soul recalls my face.
Where not even I recall a face...
Why?
The question remains in my mind.
Unanswered...
Leaving a soul of resentment.
Hatred.
How?
If you really cared
You didn't.
That's the catch.

I can't think,
Without a negative thought of you,
With each and every blink,
I'm reminded of all you don't do.
I want to be free.
I want to ignore.
I want to finally see happiness
Through another door.
I'm so miserable…
I can't focus…
Not even on me.
I'm so tired.
I just want to leave.

Who Am I?

I know a few things for sure
But it doesn't apply in your case
All the pain you had to endure…
Staring into her face.

He left on a Sunday…
I got lost in the hills,
I didn't want to come down…
The universe steered…
I tumbled to the ground…
I didn't see the light…
There was no bigger picture…
I only felt the pain…
I tried to read a scripture.

You are belligerent
Insignificant;
Lower than levels
to the ground.
I hate you.
Yet I don't.
Even if I just hope to
for a little while.
The smallest thing
brings me back.
Only to be reminded
that it'll never change.
The lies,
The broken promises,
It will always be the same.

I don't want to hate you,
But I feel I just might.
I'm doing all I can do.
It's obviously not right.
We hope.
We wish.
We pray,
For the things
That we know
Won't stay.
We beg.
We plead.
For what we want…
Trying to obtain.

Just as a python
Wrapping yourself
around my heart...
My soul...
I can't breathe.
Then you release.
But it's too late.
I can't breathe.
I can't think.
I can't live.
Not like this...
Not anymore.

The mirror faces me,
I'm undoubtedly ashamed.
My standards are adrift.
My morals? No name.
I stare into the mirror
I just don't look the same.
I'm dead but alive,
I dare speak your name.

I remember those nights when,
I cried myself to sleep.
I looked in the mirror.
And all I could see was me.
Was I not enough?
For your satisfaction…
Was I not enough?
To receive explanation…
I couldn't see past.
The smiles, the deceit.
But nothing was enough
Wasn't enough for me.

Affliction

I am alone,
In a desolate darkness
I've learned to call home
He no longer notices,
No longer cares.
So I wonder if it would
Make a difference
Me not being there.
I'm taking up space,
I'm just waiting to be told so.
Just the look in his face,
Tells me I'm getting old, I know.
What hurts the most,
Is reminiscing on our past
The way you used to love me
How we were never mad.
Unfortunately, this thing
Has taken a turn.
For some reason,
Your attention I can't earn.
But if it's the end,
It wasn't meant to be,
Just another test,
Illustrating fault in me.

One day…
One day, someone will appreciate me
And I hope it's not long.
For so long I've been trying to see,
What exactly I'm doing wrong.
Is it my face?
Body not made "just right"?
I keep running a race,
Losing, without putting up a fight.
Trying only to fail,
I gave it all to you,
Yet I still feel like I'm roaming in hell.
Sadly, you don't feel the same, too.
Sooner than later,
Tragedy will strike
I can only think of the memories,
I know it'll be something I don't like.
The worst part?
You just really don't understand
That's what breaks my heart…
You're crumbling it in your hand.

We spend so much time
Chasing what isn't there.
We've focused on the "could be"
Instead of noticing it's just not there.
Why must we as people continuously
Seek what we'll never find?
Why don't we look within ourselves?
For a constant peace of mind?
Why am I speaking to a love that's not here?
There's a continuous vacancy.
So what should I fear?
I'm near a desolate filled depression.
Is it a lesson?
Or a constant repetition of my past.
It seems to last.
I can't seem to lay it to rest.
I've literally tried my best.
It's not enough.
I'm not enough.
Will I ever be?

I live in darkness,
Surrounded by an evil entity that
I can only feel, not see.
Engorged within a world
Where I am not safe.
Scared but never attempting
To move towards the light.
Instead, I sit and rot within the sins
Of my past, of my present.
I only pray not my future as well.
I lift my hands trying to maneuver from
My current state and I see it.
Finally, I'll reach the light.
I'm almost there.
Then abruptly,
I'm stopped by an object.
Warm…
Then a whisper, your voice.
The sight of light is lost.
I'm back where I started.
You fooled me…
I can't leave.

Do you hear the beating?
Of the brick beneath your chest?
Do you feel the hate?
Building its nest?
You wonder why—
The answer is a silent cry.
Just waiting to one day die.
The past you,
The you that didn't worry
That was truly joyful inside,
That seldom cried.
She's no longer an image of you,
But will you please incorporate
Some of her traits in the future
She's dying,
And you're letting her.

Who Am I?

Seeing the dark,
No light in sight.
Steel blade on my wrist
I can't stop this.
Still cries from my heart
Won't you let me survive?
I want to feel alive...
I want to feel alive.
Help me I'm dying
Help me I'm crying
Man should I try this?
Pass it around and...
Clear.
All of my thoughts
All of my mind...
Gone.

I roll for the dead,
I roll for life.
I roll for long suffering,
I roll from my strife.
You roll around luxuries.
I've always dreamt of fame.
I wonder after this trip,
If I'll remember my name.

Who Am I?

I'm living reckless at night.
Tears from my mother—my eyes,
I just can't seem to get right…
I found a peace in,
Money, drugs, dividends
I know I'm slipping again…

Dazed

Why, oh why
Must it be this way?
I stare in the mirror,
A daze on my face.
I'm numb to reality…
A prisoner to fiction…
I pull and pull
Wanting more...
Just to mend my affliction.

Fight or flight.
The reality of life
Who knew you could
fight and lose?

You can't tell me you understand
When you've never been in my position
Constantly mouthing opinions…
Like you've ever faced opposition.
Take a walk in my shoes,
There is no park.
Wander around long enough,
You'll be alone in the dark.
See, wanderers don't follow.
If so, they cease to exist…
Wanderers beat a budding drum…
Moving at their own temp.
I don't need your lectures,
I don't need your approach.
I just need the vapors.
I pray I don't choke.

Who Am I?

Here's a list of lies I told:
I love you.
I don't care
I promise.
There's no one else.

Is it possible to return to a normal state after being shattered? Battered into a perfect mix of emotional distress.

Lost Ones

It must hurt to know
You're a lost soul…
It must hurt to realize
You're growing old.
I don't envy the dead,
Neither do I
Envy those with life.
I'm thinking of a place
Where the
Darkness turns light.
It hurts to know
I'm a lost soul,
It hurts to know
I'm growing old.
How do I stop it?

Kiyoto

I met a girl named Kiyoto,
And wouldn't you know,
She was young and vibrant,
Yet growing old.
I looked into her eyes,
I saw stars and trees,
I saw God in hell,
I saw the devil plead.
I saw famine and death,
I asked with dismay,
"Why are you doing this?"
A smile on her face.
She answered very slowly,
She told me she didn't know.
She told me there must be destruction,
In order for her to grow.

Who Am I?

She is of me,
And I am of her.
I roam in the night,
My mind won't deter.
I feel a presence in myself,
Maybe two, maybe four.
I asked them for help.
They always shut the door.
So when I pound once again,
Free of my stubborn affliction,
Will you continue to shut me out?
Or will you finally listen?
Who defines sane?
Who defines life?
Who exalts the future?
How will I take flight?

Mia A. Sims

Chapter 2:
The Awakening

Risen

The moon rises, with it me,
Gravity slowly pulls me to my eternity.
For now, I am free.
With the coming of a new moon,
My soul can finally see,
The reality, the darkness, the happiness
That life continuously brings.
I smile remembering the pain,
Emancipating myself from the rain,
It was all worth it.
My soul so contingent.
I'd prayed for this moment.
This moment of self recognition,
God took me through all those storms,
So that I'd finally listen.

I finally understand it all,
And I can tell you so.
With the rising of this new moon,
Rises my new soul.
I rise with the waves,
The waves of eternity,
I rise within this moment of bliss,
That the world will never see.
Only me—my special place.
All those people…
Who took advantage of me,
Finally erased.
You could never understand,
A girl with the world in her hands,
Manipulated into corruption,
But that deterioration could never last.
I rose. I continue to rise.

Substitute Part I

In contemplation of my options,
I refused to choose.
You see, choosing was losing,
And I couldn't fathom the concept of lose.
To substitute my affliction,
I replaced it with a new addiction.
Love is all you need,
But its substitute set me free.
See life can throw it's never ending obstacles,
As humans, the pressure is just a seed;
It grows and expands into insecurities,
That for some reason never seem to leave.
Those insecurities obviously fears,
Fears compromising dreams,
Dreams turning into nightmares,
Nightmares captivating the ability to see.
The. Pressure.
   Redundant to voice its sadistic hold on peers,
But there is a calming voice in the vapors,
This feeling could last for years…
Maybe months… Maybe weeks,
Maybe a day…. Or so.
With this revolving evolution,
It's hard to really know.

Substitute Part II

You're exhausted with life,
Me too, I know.
Let's allow the intertwining of our spirits,
I don't want your heart,
Give me your soul.
Your physical attributes are an addition,
This substitute shows me so,
Lost in its simplistic beauty,
I just need to know…
Are you ready?
According to the sins of the past,
You are, me too.
But before energies reach their peak,
Let's embrace this substitute.
We'll float with the wind,
Soar through the clouds,
Make it up to Heaven,
Will we ever come down?
Let's rid our hearts of hate,
Love conquers,
It reveals the truth…
But then sometimes it's a bit predictable,
Let's stick to the substitute.

Life

The truth in life is this:
It's not always filled with bliss.
It's filled with deception,
An abundance of pain,
Sometimes no sunshine, only rain.
I cried for so many seasons…
And only I knew the reason.
Wandering in a world so new,
Relying on the wrong things,
To get me through.
I knocked at the Devil's door,
And he answered me with a tour,
An invitation to keep rotting,
Until there was no more.
At first the life was substantial,
I kept feeding my addiction,
To belong, to matter, to be loved,
Continuously fueling my affliction.
But then it sucked me dry,
Until I was no more,
Robbing me of innocence,
Keeping me in its lure.
In this spectrum there is no life,
No happiness, only pain.
I cried remembering the sunshine,
Somehow I embraced the rain.

Who Am I?

The truth in life is this,
It's not always filled with bliss,
Sometimes it's just a mockery,
A mockery that you exist.
But that's the moment you close your eyes,
Pray for meekness, Pray for strength.
Pray for deliverance from that hell,
Pray He'll always be fence.

Repetition is the key
To insanity,
Driving the same trails,
Doing so sporadically.
Hearing the same old phrase
At a quarter past 2:
"I wonder if there's more tea."
I wonder about the truth
I wonder about the future.
Dammit, I have goals.
I'm tired of slaving at a 9-5.
Fuck this, I want more.

I Wonder

Sometimes I stare into space,
Wondering is it true—
My life of continuous lose…
Was it me? Or was it you?
Was it the things I didn't do?
For you? For them?
What the corruption of the world will do.
I never grew or so I thought,
I was just wandering,
Never was I lost.
The truth obtained but at a cost.
Life sold me, shaped me, molded me,
Bought me back again.
The irony – an innocent little girl,
Fascinated by a world of sin.
But she'd win,
Even though she didn't know.
It wasn't you, wasn't them…
It was her,
She had to grow.
The mirror faces me,
As I look into my own eyes.
"I'm fine."
No more little girl.
Maturity slowly reaching its peak,
There's an appreciation for the struggle.
That's the only way it can be beat.
I know me.

There's a secret in this life,
The key is being you,
Understanding your importance,
In all that you do.
They'll lie, they'll despise,
They'll tear you in two,
Keep your eye on the prize though,
Do this for you.
People won't understand you,
For that, they'll criticize,
You'll have friends turn to foes,
Right before your eyes.
You'll have no power over them,
Or the evil things they do,
There's a secret in your struggling,
The key is being you.

Dry your eyes, never let up,
Tupac spoke those words true,
Keep your head up through it all,
Continue being you.
Yeah, people are evil.
They'll do things you won't understand.
But you must realize the power to overcome,
Lies right in the palms of your hands.
Let them talk. They'll never stop.
Applauding will start when you reach the top.
They'll hate and dream of tearing you in two,
But you finally made it out.
The key was being you.

Slaves to Society

A disgrace to the races,
Why we paint our faces,
To maintain the hype,
We remain a stereotypical type.
We fight, we lose, we choose,
This misery.
Is this the way they'd want us to be?
I mean Dr. King, Malcom X,
Medgar Evers and Rosa…
They fought for our liberty,
What do we have to show for it?
Emancipate yourselves,
Slavery is growing old but relevant.
It's a mental, emotional,
and political crisis now,
People just won't accept it.
We won't stop,
We're attracted to the diamonds.
"Bruh where'd you get that watch?"
Girls screaming look at all he got,
Misunderstanding their value,
So they're labeled a "thot."

What's wrong with this age?
They kill us like we're runaway slaves.
Gunning us down two by two,
If you're not careful it could be you.
They take our money,
Exploitation for capital gain,
And right before change takes place,
We continue to remain the same.
The corruption and hate,
Remains the cause of our fate.
God give us your grace,
We may not see the next day.
Help us.

It was the music that connected us.
Our upbringing even more.
A trailer home,
We dreamt of domes.
We'll make it there for sure.
I remember talks of private jets,
Owning businesses, stocks and more.
I remember when we lost touch.
Felt it in my core.
And your spirit I still feel
Though your skin I can't touch.
We were caught up in the motion.
Didn't really think so much.
You were mine,
If only for a while
I was yours,
You made me smile.
Goodbye good friend,
I wish you well.
I'll continue prayer
for your prosperity.
Only time will tell.

Danger is only a word.
A fear I don't possess.
I come alive in the wake
Of distress.
Take my hand and teach me.
I'd let you go if you leave me.
But for now,
Let's lie.
Let's forget our troubles.
Erase our lives.
Yours with her…
Mine with them.
I was a floating bubble of mess.
You reeled me in.
You are that light and darkness,
A necessity to sustain.
I understand 'be careful what you wish for'
Though I didn't wish your name…
My youth overbearing,
Risking it all for a day…
I try to voice my thoughts,
But can't form words to say.

Lost Angels

They all came here to be famous...
No one knows what their name is...
They'll fight until poverty-stricken...
Paint and sing as if no one's listening.
They are the angels of the coast...
The place I love most...
I have hope.
The artist who's bold—
With those filth-filled clothes...
Painting, drumming, dancing...
Embracing...
Long live the Lost Angels...
No one knows what their name is...
But I see your soul.
You will rise.

Black spotted butterfly
Oh me oh my…
I think I caught a butterfly
But for some reason,
It wouldn't stay long.
I decided to help...
Sing it a song.
It didn't listen…
It flew away
It's blue covered wing
Batting my face…

9-5

I'm sitting at a desk…
Praying for the next…
Why didn't they tell me about life?
That I'd work and slave—
I was best behaved…
I wonder what it feels like
To be rich…
Not in health, I have that.
Not in life, I was blessed with that.
but money…
The root of all evil my mom would say.
Why is it then,
That's the first thing churches want in the tray?
Why is it that I must have it to survive?
It's my only option if I wish to stay alive.
I'd love to live in the trees…
Without my physical— just me
I'd love to get lost in the waves…
Only to rise above them
Once again.
I'm sitting at a desk,
Praying for what's next.
I have a sad reality:
The next is yet to come.

Who Am I?

I just want what
Everyone's fiending for
Not lust, not sex—
I want more.
Can I rant about my dreams?
Then listen to you rant yours?
Can we simply hold each other
While the rest of the world is ignored?
Can I cry when I'm angry?
Vent when I'm upset?
Will you tell me "babe it'll be OK"?
Or turn your back then regret?
I want the endless talks at night.
I want to someday reminisce…
Of our good, our bad
The reason this bond still exists.
I want to build a foundation
A place where I fear less
 A foundation our children will see
 So that they'll be open to only the best.
I don't want to miss you
I want you to be right here.
No more lies, no more hate.
Hold me tight, no more fears.
I want what we dream of
And I pray it still exits
I want you, I want me, US.
A love that never quits.

I cried and cried,
I didn't know why,
I wept for a purpose,
I wanted to die.
I leapt for a light
That I wanted to shine.
I closed my eyes,
It was in my mind.
I wanted a change,
But I just couldn't see...
The change I needed,
Was inside me.

My most precious gift
Life itself is the most precious gift of all.
Until those times when I suddenly fall
Looking around for answers
That don't seem to exist.
Then praying for just one wish
Unfortunately wishes aren't real
I stop to question if the gift of life
Is it precious or worth a kill?

I love thee with a love I seemed ,
To lose with my lost saints.
I lie here thinking of you,
Though flames burn at his flesh,
Though poison will pour from his tongue.
Though this is a trap for fools.
I love the foolery.

Summer nights in country fields
Rolling around the way.
I got lost inside your eyes,
I wanted you to stay.
I still remember that December,
The only thing so real.
You were mine
And I was yours…
Roaming in the hills.

I look around and see white,
Not a burst of color in sight.
I feel like I'm in outer space.
All my people took flight.
If they erase us from the media,
But drown us all in fame.
The future generations will only know
Manipulated black names.
"We love to showcase minorities"
keep the lies to yourself.
Keep your promises,
My humbleness,
Is truly a gifted cry for help.
I look around and see white.
Not a burst of color in sight.
They'd erase us if they could.
Binding us to their hoods.

Maybe I would've fit in,
If I was a little darker—
As if the color of my skin
Is a true color marker.
As if my grandmother's body
Wasn't taken against her will…
As if his blood doesn't run
Through my pale light skin.
That man is a rapist.
And he is a piece of me.
The sins of their fathers.
In nearly every inch of me.
I hated myself for so long.
But I am not to blame.
It is the sins of their father…
I wish I knew his name.

I'm tired of demands
From hopeless, tired sheep
Who work for billionaires.
Whose noses flare
If they even make a peep.
"Do this, do that"
As if they're really in control.
Not even realizing
They are the maker's mold.
Slaves to their ignorance
They should all be ashamed.
But I don't even blame them.
They don't know their own names.

Why did I choose this path?
I swear I do not know.
I could've done the math
To know this would
Wear on my soul.
Where is the culture?
Lost amidst the wind…
We fight so very hard
And they won't let us win.
Win or lose
I have a goal
I'll see that it's reached.
I don't want to
be in a classroom,
But I know that I will teach.

Don't trust a soul.
Don't trust what you see.
Don't trust the helpful smiles.
Don't even trust me.
You should question all information,
The media is corrupt.
I know for myself.
I've seen it enough.
I'm done with the lies.
If they won't let me,
I'll scream the truth.
I'll leave a legacy after death.
I'll still inform the youth.

Little Sadie wants to be free,
She wants to roam with me...
She wants to roam in the physical,
Her spirit bound no leave.
She asked me how it was out there,
I shrugged, told her "OK"
She frowned. She snarled.
She was confused.
She no longer wanted to play.
I asked her why she was angry
Her eyes blood red, stained.
She told me I was ungrateful...
That I didn't deserve to stay.

Mia A. Sims

.

Chapter 3:
Freedom

Free

"Bed Peace," and memories,
Driving along the way.
Warm nights and blue skies,
Fill her chuckling face…
She takes pleasure in dark measures.
She's not really sane…
She's not what we're asking for…
Throw filth on her name.
She's young.
And free.
But see...
She's me
She's home
Indeed
With me…
I'm free.

Dreamer

Whoever said,
That the dreams,
Of the dreamers are dead?
Who curses their efforts
and prays they shed?
Why are we drawn
to the evil within?
When the light within us
is begging a chance.
I prayed for understanding,
I prayed for rain
I prayed for solace,
I prayed for change.
I pray for you—times are bad.
If I can help,
Give me your hand.
I know times are hard...
Understand it gets tough,
But keep on going
Even when enough is enough
Because there is a truth in this life
Many don't know it exists...
But if you ever find it,
Your soul will be at rest.

I remember it all…
Young, dumb, and willing.
Listening to every sweet whisper,
Not knowing,
Experiencing too much.
Too young.
Naïve.
Hope arrived in the end.
A light that was always there.
Was finally seen.
No more tears
No more stress
Again...
A new beginning.

1-4-12

Writing poetry helps me escape reality. I enter a world of my own where nothing and no one else matters. Only me and my thoughts. Music does the same— whether it's the bass, the solemn voice who sings of her broken heart, or the tranquil flow—an escape from reality that I frequently need. both music and writing are there when I feel alone with no one to turn to.

Shimmering just as the sun
off the waves
Of a beautiful sea—
It stands,
Though not just in one place.
I am surrounded
By millions of these glowing objects
Observing then obtaining.
I am in love.

Lying so still,
Yet moving arms
and legs frequently.
Graceful.
The little angel sleeps.
So innocent
So pure…
God's gift to the earth.

You bring light to
My darkened room
On a cloudy day
You'd still bloom
You are my angel—
Heaven sent, just for me
I embrace your indifference
I beg of you,
Don't leave.
What a surprise
What a shame
You came into my life
No given name
We roamed, and loved
And reached heaven above
When we descended
It didn't end it…
Though I pity her fate.
Maybe you'll go,
Maybe you'll stay.
In this moment,
Lay.

There is a darkness
Fixed in bliss.
It's almost sickening
It exists.
It corrupts the minds
Of the young and old.
Tearing through cities
Snatching souls.
You can't fight
What you don't see,
But why do I feel
So much power in me?
Why do if feel
I could defeat the roaring beast?
It's because I'm covered
With blood from a
High reigning priest.

I lose myself in these hills
Each time I roam
My mind, my heart
Singing an everlasting song.
The Lost Angels
Of Los Angeles,
Constantly calling to me.
Are they asking me to be?
What I've always dreamt to see?
I know greater is coming,
The coast guides my reason.
I'll roam and love in this moment
I know soon it will be my season.

Palms trees
and ocean breezes,
Blowing with the wind.
I smile. a trial.
I'll try a dose of sin.
How can it be wrong?
When it feels so right…
I'll try a few doses of sin.
If only for a night.

My hair blows in the wind.
And it all finally makes sense.
Life, trials, trouble, pain,
My choice of self-defense.
The truth comes alive here.
I feel like I know.
No rain, only sunshine,
No trouble anymore.

Red bull and vapors
Rolling on this road trip.
I've grown to love it—
Traveling with no tips.
They ask me why I go alone.
"Are you not afraid?"
I roam into the unknown…
No thoughts on my brain.
I encourage you to try it.
Live a little. Fly.

A fly on the wall
Could tell you all my secrets.
I'm thankful to God
They don't have voices
To feed it…
Their questions.
Their blame…
Am I crazy?
Am I sane?
It is for me to decide.
And that's just it.
A fly on the wall.
Would tell all of it.

Who Am I?

Life is but a dream
Filled with wondrous things.
I remember dreading the sunrise,
Now I see heaven in those skies.
I was once lost,
And now I'm found.
I was once disturbed,
I am now sound.

Fly little bird
And don't you let them
Hear a peep.
Tell those who are suffering,
They are not their trembling sheep.
Fly to the mountains
Bring your wisdom back down.
Know when you rest
You'll finally wear the crown.

Thank you for impurity,

Thank you for the pain.

Thank you for the sunshine

Thank you for the rain.

I fell in love on a Sunday,

And lost it all by noon.

Strutting on life's runway,

I wanted it all too soon.

I dance beneath the stars,

I sing amidst the blue.

Thank you for long suffering.

Thank you for the truth.

If I grew wings today
Would I just fly away?
Or would I lie and
Absorb the waves?
Floating from existence
With so many words to say.
Yet no messages to relay.
Should I stay?

It's hard to see
Without direction.
It's hard to feel—
Love, protection.
It's hard to compromise,
Somehow I do.
It's hard to love you.
But you are the truth.

The leaves on the trees
Look so different today.
I stare, feeling the breeze.
I know no delay.
My hands look different
Yesterday I was much older.
Yesterday I was strong,
I was much colder.
The flowers in the grass,
Don't bloom the way they did.
I remember dancing in those lilies,
As a silly little kid.
Everything is changing…
And I too have evolved.
Life looks so different today.
I feel I can have it all.

Who Am I?

Yes, I called to the wind

And I felt deserving of an answer

Entitlement isn't heaven-sent

It's an ugly disaster.

Don't expect too much,

Don't take too little.

Don't beg for a chance,

Don't sell yourself brittle.

I call to the wind,

I'd have you know she responded.

She told me take a deep breath,

The pressure is upon you.

Get ready for a ride,

One you will surely

One day miss.

Get ready for the ride.

A ride of rightful bliss.

My future is ahead,

The past is a fluke.

I laugh thinking of cries.

I laugh thinking of you.

I remember those sleepless nights.

Drinking, smoking,

Four by two.

I thought the answer was in your eyes.

The trouble was always you.

I no longer whine for your love.

I only whine seeking truth.

I no longer think of your despair.

Or your draining of my youth.

She is free,
And she is me,
She is floating
Effortlessly.
I see no worry,
I see no pain,
I see sunshine.
I embrace the rain.
Ancestors pass.
I continue to grow.
Their everlasting spirit
Waning on my bountiful soul.

My Father in Heaven,
If you are a man,
You've raised the toll.
If you are a woman,
I understand.
Why I feel so whole.
I now know the shocking truth—
That most things don't exist.
We are what we are not.
You've helped me see this.
So my spiritual guider in Nirvana,
Won't you guide me towards the light?
Won't you see that my purpose is filled.
That Mary has delight.
She wanted me to be big.
I told her I'd do it all.
I pray for your continued guidance.
Please don't let me fall.

We danced erratically,
Like devils in the wind.
I saw you…
You saw me.
You wouldn't let me in.
I banged at the door,
And an angel appeared.
I saw light in your dark eyes,
I saw pain in those tears.
I held you,
Loved you,
And cherished you.
I will never be ashamed.
In the hazy fall of nighttime,
I always remember your name.

Never thought
In a million years,
I could feel so alive.
The pain, the worries,
I embrace it as I fly.
You cannot tear apart,
What has already been torn.
You cannot wear down,
What has already been worn.
I cried in the nighttime.
I cried for days.
I awoke on a mountain.
My mind a complete haze.
I laughed as a maniac,
Desperate for his first kill.
I laughed thinking of the future.
I danced in the hills.
I wanted a bit of solace.
Then came only rain.
I embraced the somber thoughts.
I no longer feel pain.
I'm numb to the lies,
Aware of the truth.
I never thought in a million years,
I'd be right here with you.

Hello, my dear,
It's been another year…
Somehow you've stayed afloat.
You blossomed like a tulip,
Lips like Cool Whip,
A numbing taste for the old.
I see you clearly,
And I hear your mind.
I'm watching your footsteps,
Just take your time.
You're a dangerous little thing
Always stay silent.
Keep them on their toes.
Don't promote violence.

Lightening in the sky,
Wetness in the breeze...
I dance amongst the clouds...
I do only as I please.
I scream in laughter...
I roll along the leaves,
I'm a filthy disaster...
I don't care if the world sees.

Who Am I?

I heard a whisper in the mountains,
It came amidst the breeze,
It asked me what I was doing there.
I said, "roaming as I please."
It laughed and whirled around me,
I felt warm, happy, finally at peace
I turned to see my grandmother
Smiling out at me.

Hello young wanderer,
How does it feel?
To finally walk in light.
All the darkness,
World of pompous,
No longer your delight.
You laugh and sing,
And speak of dreams,
I envy your love for life.
But I take good care,
Make sure you're aware.
You'll never endure that strife.

Yes, my love,
You made it through.
I've walked this path
With you.
They didn't know,
They wouldn't listen.
Turned their noses,
Burned their bridges.
The truth has set you free,
As I told you it would.
The ancestors are calling.
For your success…
Your good.
So run little angel.
And please,
Don't cry.
Run away from danger.
Tell them I said hi.
We can't walk,
You're drifting,
And I cannot hide.
We can't feel
In the physical.
But one day we will fly.

I am free.
I know who I am.

Original Works
Circa 2012-14

Mia A. Sims

I wanted to showcase a few of my poems I wrote while in high school in raw form. I've written poetry, short stories and songs for years—since I was in fourth grade—but I sadly couldn't dig up any from that long ago. I wanted to share what I do have. My family and I found these in my childhood home. Many of them are originals of poems included in this book.

We spend so much time chasing what isn't there. We've focused on the "could be" instead of noticing its just not here. Why must we as people continuously seek what we'll never find? Why don't we look within ourselves for a constant piece of mind. Why am I speaking to a love that's not here? There's a vacancy so what should I fear? I'm near... a desolate filled depression. Is it a lesson? Or a constant repetition... of my past It seems to last. I can't seem to lay it at rest. I've literally tried my best. It's not enough. I'm not enough. Will I ever be?

The more there's hate;
The more there's love.
I pull harder,
You continue to shove.
I cry,
You don't.
I try,
You won't.
The moment I smile,
You turn it around.
Are you doing it on purpose?
Guess I'll see in a while.
So much convincing,
from me to myself,
But my hope is sinking,
I just need your help.
Wish I would open my eyes,
Simply just to see
The only person who really cares,
Is me.

A Love That Never Quits

I just want what everyone's fiending for.
Not lust, Not sex.
I want more.
Can I rant about my dreams?
Then listen to you rant yours?
Can we simply hold each other,
while the rest of the world is
ignored.
Can I cry when I'm angry?
Vent when I'm upset?
Will you tell me "babe, it'll be ok
Or turn your back and then regret.
I want the endless talks at night,
I want to someday reminisce;
Of our good, our bad,
The reason this bond still exists.
I want to build a foundation
Of hope, of care,
A place where I fear less,
A foundation our children will see,
So that they'll be open to only
The best.
I don't wanna miss you;
I want you to be right here.
No more lies, no more hate.
Hold me tight, no more fear.
I want what we dream of,

Who Am I?

What you've done in your past has nothing to do with what is going on now. it only reminds you of the mistakes you've made to not be made again. Don't reflect on the past to torture yourself but instead to better yourself.

One day someone will appreciate me,
And I hope it's not long.
For so long I've been trying to see,
what exactly I'm doing wrong.

Is it my face?
Body not made "just right?"
I keep running a race...
Losing, without putting up a fight.

Trying only to learn fail.
Gave it all to you,
Yet I still feel like I'm roaming in hell.
Sadly, you don't feel the same too.

Sooner than later,
Tragedy will strike,
I can only think of the memories.
I know it'll be something I don't like:

The worst part?
You just really don't understand.
That's what breaks my heart...
You're crumbling it in your hand.

Who Am I?

Cry child cry,
For you're the only one who can hear yourself
weep.
Cry child cry,
I know the rocky mountains in life have gotten so
steep.
Cry child cry,
See if anyone cares,
Ask "them" for help w/ your problems,
They wouldn't dare.
Cry child cry,
Tell the story of a lost soul,
Tell of the sight of horror,
That made you so cold.
Cry child cry,
If no one hears you I can,
Only because those tears,
Are right in the palms of my hands.

Love, hope;
hell, dispair.
searching for redemption,
But how redeemer is near.
Calling to the dark,
Encouraging more demons to enact.
Preparing to battle,
only to never react.
Promises, care.
why were you never there?
Desolation, the cold...
why do you remain in my soul?

Who Am I?

I live in darkness,
surrounded by an evil entity that
I can only feel; not see.
Engorged within a world where I am not safe.
Scared but never attempting to move towards
the light.
Instead, I sit and rot within the sins of
my past, my present....
I only pray not my future as well.
I lift my hands, trying to manuever from
the ~~a~~ my current state... I see it.
~~I feel as though~~, Finally, I'll reach the light,
I'm almost there.
Then abruptly I'm stopped by an object.
Warm.
Then a whisper, your voice....
The sight of light is lost....
I'm back where I started...
~~Getting from the~~ you fooled me...
I can't leave...

I am alone...
In a desolate darkness I've learned to call home.
He no longer notices, he no longer cares.
So I wonder if it would make a difference,
Me not being there.
I'm taking up space,
I'm just waiting to be told so.
Just the look in his face,
Tells me this has gotten old, I know.
What hurts the most,
Is reminiscing on our past,
The way you used to love me,
How we were never mad.
Unfortunately this thing has taken a turn,
For some reason it's his attention I can't earn.
But if it's the end,
It just wasn't meant to be.
Just another test,
Illustrating the fault in me.

Who Am I?

Just wanna move away,
So far I'm forgotten,
So far not a soul recalls my face,
Where not even I recall a face,
Why?
The question remains in my mind
Unanswered.
Leaving with a soul of resentment,
Hatred.
How?
If you really cared?
You didn't.
That's the catch.

We pray and pray for a change
when we all know we wanna stay the same
we just wanna stop
we keep on going
through a lot in
takes on growing
we not even for a second do
we not to think...
but reality

takes a serious mind
to completely mend a heart
so take your time,
if you want a new start
be real with yourself,
who you wanna be?
keep lying to yourself, one day you're
gonna see... it wasn't worth it...
But you ask yourself... was it all worth
it, will it ever be?
stays the same...
will it ever change

Who Am I?

I remember it all...
Young, dumb, and willing,
Listening to every sweet whisper,
Not knowing...
Experiencing too much...
Too young...
Nieve...
Hopelessness arrived in the end...
A light that was always there
was finally paid attention to..
No more tears...
No more sadness...
Again...
A new beginning.

I remember those nights when
I cried myself to sleep,
I, I looked in the mirror,
And all I could see was me
Was I not enough,
For your satisfaction?
Was I not enough,
To receive explanation
I couldn't see past,
The smiles the deceit,
But nothing was enough,
wasn't enough for me

Shhh...
Do you hear the beating
of the brick beneath your chest?
Do you feel the hate
building its nest?
You wonder why,
The answer is a silent cry
Just waiting to one day die.
The past you,
The you that didn't worry,
That was truly joyful inside,
That seldomly cried.
She's no longer an image of you...
But will you please incorporate
some of her traits in her future.
She's dying, And you're letting her.

I was completely torn...
like you... my family... who
which meant so damn much to me.
my mother ... was soo disappointed in me
couldn't even look to me.
living in the same home
felt so alone...
I swear I couldn't breathe.
took every when of life out of me
I wasn't even me...
But we got back right; regained my
life...
refuse to let ya kill me.

Though you nearly killed me
Mentally, emotionally,
I regained my stability.
Lord knows I hated you
for everything you did to me...
But I opened my eyes to see

Who Am I?

Tell me where do you go
when hell is all you know.
Helplessly walking because you're
walking completely blind...
Trying to erase the thoughts,
But they won't clear your mind.
Soft whispers encouraging on to kill,
This evil state of mind just doesn't
seem real.
Who understands what is diagnosed
as insanity?
Fighting to be common just as the
rest of humanity.
Make it stop...
Slowly rip it from my head,
So that once it is gone;
It will surely remain dead.

I can't think,
without a negative thought of you,
whoreo with each & every blink,
I'm reminded of all you DON'T do.
I want to be free,
I want to ignore,
I want to finally see,
Happiness through another door.
I'm so miserable I can't focus
not even on me,
I'm so tired.
I want to leave

How to find Love the Right Way

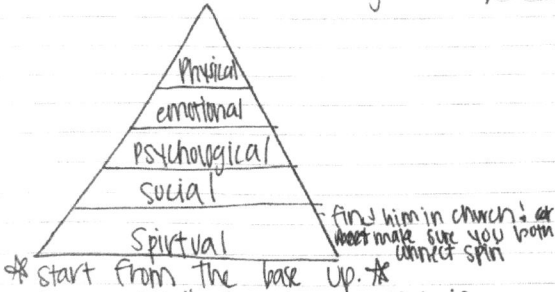

Physical
emotional
psychological
social
Spiritual

— find him in church; or
meet mate sure you both
connect spin

* Start from the base up. *

How can a relationship be successful if you don't connect in more ways than physically first?

God's Prescription for _Successful_ Relationships
1) Become the right person
2) Walk in love instead of "falling in love"
3) Fix your hope on God and seek to please him through this relationship.
4) If failure occurs, repeat steps 1, 2, & 3

1-3-12

My most precious gift...
Life itself is usually the most precious gift of all,
Until those times when I suddenly fall,
Looking around for answers that don't seem
to exist.
Then praying for just one wish.
Unfortunately wishes are not real,
I stop to question if the gift of life is
precious or worth a kill.
Then I raise my eyes to the sky,
Not daring to ask why.
For He makes no mistakes, he's perfect indeed.
His guidance through trials is the only thing
I need.
Life itself is definitely the most precious gift
of all.
Because even when it gets me down, God
is there to pick me up from the fall.

I cried and cried,
I didn't know why,
I wept for a purpose,
I wanted to die,
I lept for a light
That I wanted to shine
I closed my eyes
It was in my mind.
I wanted a change,
But I just couldn't see,
The evolution I needed,
Lied in Thee.
I begged for forgiveness,
He heard my prayers,
I am at peace,
And He is there.

Mia A. Sims

The door is closed; But the curiosity within me begged to creep
A cloud of fog bursts from within.
I slam it shut; yet still curious.
Slowly reopening I see light,
But not just any kind of light, it held joy.
As I approached, the warmness that it
created gave me hope.
For what exactly I don't know.
Closing my eyes, I stretch my hand forward,
Something grabs me and lures me in,
I no longer feel the warmth,
As I open my eyes to face the coldness that
now conceals my hand,
I see a collage of everything I'd tried to forget.
There's no running away;
It is there forever

Who Am I?

1-9-12

Writing poetry helps me escape reality. I enter a world of my own where nothing and no one else matters; only me and my thoughts. Music does the same. Whether it's the bass, the solumn voice who sings of her broken heart, or the tranquil flow. Both music and writing are there when I feel alone, with no one to turn to. I feel so alone; so safe.
An escape from reality, which I frequently need.

1-6-12

Darkness...
From the depths of an unknown world,
It slowly rises; soaring for its prey.
winding from tunnels below streets,
To ^alleys kept hushed from the children of priests.
Creeps ~~slyly~~ from the closet,
Watches them sleep,
bares them to open their eyes.
Manuevers its wrath ~~into the mind of~~
Into the mind of the innocent,
~~~~~~ Rips them of purity,
forcing a soul of sin; desperate for the kill.

Who Am I?

1) Shimmering just as the sun off the waves of a
beautiful sea,
It glares.
Though not just in one place.
I am surrounded by, drawn slowly
by millions of these glowing objects.
revolving them, obtaining
I am in love.

2) Lying so still,
his legs, arms and legs frequently,
Beautiful,
A little angel sleeps.
So innocent,
So pure...
God's gift to the earth.

3) You are belligerent.
Insignificant;
Lower than level to the ground.
I hate you;
Yet, I don't.
Even if I just hoped to for a little while.
The smallest thing brings me back,
Only to be reminded that it'll never change.

Mia A. Sims

1-12-12

Torn between two... And then I had to choose. You see, that's what hurts the most... The fact that I chose you. And I was so hesitant at first, then I gave in. Gave in to the charade that you kept going for so long. You lied, pretended, like it was nothing; only to rip my heart right from my chest. And yea, I've been through it before but with you? My best friend? The only person I felt I could really count on? How could you? Now all I do is sit and think, trying to understand where I went wrong, what I did wrong... How much harder could I have tried? Feels like half of me has completely died. I sit and think... Put myself into my own pool of misery, just thinking. And Not only do I have to deal with up reality awake but also as I sleep. Don't even like to sleep anymore. Haven't really been eating much either... But you'll never know. Yea And you'll never understand. And I say I don't care but... It's ridiculous. The one person who said they'd always be there was never actually there at all. And so that makes

Who Am I?

The lies,
The broken promises,
It will always be the same
Just as a python...
4/ wrapping yourself around my heart,
My soul,
~~Until~~ I can't breathe. ~~Then you rel~~
Then you release,
But it's too late.
I can't breathe,
I can't think,
I can't live,
Not like this.
Not anymore.

Runs...

oh I'm
Just sitting,
Just waiting,
Just praying,
For a change,
Then you moved up.
You glowed up my world.
Been watching you,
damn now stalking you,
for sure.

Yeah

Seeing the dark, no light,
Steel blade on my wrist,
I can't stop this,
Still cries from my heart,
won't you let me survive,
I want to feel alive,
I want to feel alive

Help me I'm dying,
Help me I'm crying,
Mah should I try this?
Pass it around and...
Clear,
All of my thoughts
All of my mind,
I don't have time

ABOUT THE AUTHOR

A native of Mississippi, Sims discovered her capability to express art through words at the age of 9-years-old. A graduate of the University of Mississippi, she's worked as a reporter, both full-time and freelance, a songwriter, and poet. She enjoys green tea, road trips and walks along the beach.